A LE[...] TREATISE OF THE PLAGUE

A LEARNED TREATISE OF THE PLAGUE

Wherein the two questions:
Whether the Plague be Infectious, or no

&

Whether and how far it may be shunned of Christians by
going aside are resolved

THEODORE BEZA

CANON PRESS

MOSCOW, IDAHO

Published by Canon Press
P.O. Box 8729, Moscow, Idaho 83843
800-488-2034 | www.canonpress.com

A Learned Treatise of the Plague
©2020 Ben Castle. Translated by Edward Percival in 1665.

Library of Congress Cataloging-in-Publication Data is forthcoming.

20 21 22   3 2 1

INTRODUCTION

THEODORE BEZA (June 24, 1519 – October 13, 1605) was a Reformed theologian who took over the spiritual leadership of Geneva upon the death of John Calvin. The work before you was one of his many productions and it deals with the ethical duties of a Christian during an outbreak of the plague. In the body of the treatise, there is no mention of an actual outbreak, which makes it difficult to identify which outbreak of the plague Beza was writing about. The preface to the 1665 edition (the edition upon which this is based) indicates that a Mr. Edward Percival published Beza's *Of the Plague* in London in 1665, the Plague Year. Whatever the occasion for the original work of Beza, Mr. Percival thought it worthy of republication in his day.

With the outbreak of the coronavirus strain COVID-19, the Church is forced to ask questions we have not had to face since the recurring outbreaks of the bubonic plague. The Plague ran through several epidemics during the Middle Ages and continued up to the year 1665 in England. The questions the Church is facing now are the same questions faced by Beza and Mr. Percival, and it is the wisdom of the Church to listen to her forefathers in the faith. Since Beza's day, the responsibilities of the Church haven't changed. The relation between the sovereignty of God, the duties incumbent upon Christians, the relative wisdom and morality of quarantine or "turning aside" (as Beza phrases it), and the role of the magistrate during an outbreak are all on the table once again. The primary focus of Beza's work and the chief source of our moral reasoning in times of outbreak is the relation between the primary cause of all that comes to pass and the secondary causes by which they fall out. The Westminster Confession of Faith, Chapter 3, paragraph 1 says:

> God, from all eternity, did, by the most wise and holy counsel of his own will, freely, and unchangeably ordain whatsoever comes to pass: yet so, as thereby neither is God the author of sin, nor is violence offered to the will of the creatures; *nor is the liberty or contingency of second causes taken away, but rather established.*

This paragraph is teaching that, even though all things that happen do so because God decreed them to happen, they still occur according to the nature of cause and effect. Bullets cause wounds. If you are shot with a gun, you will probably get a serious wound. This effect (your wound) comes about through the cause of being shot. This whole chain of cause (being shot) and effect (being wounded) is part of God's eternal decree. But, and this is the key point, the bullet and the wound it can cause are secondary to the decree. While God's decree is the primary cause, this does not take away the fact that the bullet is the secondary cause. This means that a wound may be caused by a bullet according to God's eternal decree, but that event is contingent on the freely chosen actions of creatures. Many a tale of the forgotten Zippo in the G.I.'s breast pocket illustrates the contingent nature of secondary causes. And it is the gray area between the primary cause (God's decree) and the various secondary causes (viruses, bullets, moral duties, etc) by which things happen in our lives that gives rise to the ethical dilemma Beza handles in this treatise. The outbreak of COVID-19 presents this dilemma to us once again. The contingency of secondary causes gives rise to what we call risk. And it is in the realm of risk that our current moral reasoning, from both church and state, is in dire need of guidance from Beza. The relation between the eternal, unchangeable, and fixed decree of God and the contingent nature of second causes is one of the perennial problems of Western philosophy and theology. And it is here that the Church, as the pillar and ground of the truth (1 Timothy 3:15), must speak.

There are, however, things in Beza's treatise that will seem odd to modern readers. He was a man of his time, and he held certain assumptions about medicine and astrology that the modern world has abandoned. Keep in mind, however, that to reason about secondary causes in relation to the primary cause does not commit one to an exclusive account of those secondary causes. What Beza calls a "corruption of the humors," we call a "viral infection." What he calls a "corruption of the air," we call an "airborne virus." What was called a "certain placing of the stars," we call a "correlation." Don't let the differing account of the secondary causes in particular prevent you from learning about secondary causes in general, since in every age any account of secondary causes is provisional, including ours. In every age, our account of the primary cause and its relation to secondary causes is certain and sure, even as the Word of God is sure and certain, since it is from the Word that we know about the primary cause. And just as that Word has not changed, though all the world has, so also the dependence of secondary causes upon the primary cause will never change. It is in this confidence that we can discern our duty, for the liberty and contingency of second causes is not taken away, but rather established by God's decree.

In this edition, I have worked from the English translation of Beza's Latin original. My goal has been to clear up the Latinate syntax of the 1665 edition for ease of comprehension among modern readers. I have added Scripture references where they were lacking and formatted Beza's where they depart from modern conventions. I have also added footnotes to clarify Beza's meaning and to try and clear up his polemic style, as well as punctuation.

That this learned treatise proves helpful to you and your congregation in navigating these uncertain times is the prayer of

Your humble servant,
Ben Castle, pastor of Grace OPC, Lynchburg, VA.
March 2020.

DEDICATION

To the Honorable Sir John Robinson,

Lieutenant of His Majesty's Principal Fortress, the Tower of London,

Honorable Sir, the confidence of a stranger will, I hope, easily meet your pardon, when the worth of the author, and the occasional subject of the discourse (in these contagious and calamitous times) have given me too sad an opportunity of presenting it to your honor, whose concerns for the public welfare, (even in this Great City) are as eminently great as any others. The matter of the discourse is a confutation and reconciling of the only two destructive opinions which in all ages (in contagious and infectious times) have ever proved fatal to the world. The one, too much presuming and relying upon this bold opinion, that the plague is not infectious. And the other[1], out of a weak and unspirited precipitation, [that all] without exception, fly away from it. Both of which are

---

1. What Beza's opponents mean by "particular" (or "several" in the 1665 edition) is that each one contracts a disease immediately (without secondary causes) from the judgment of God. They prefer this opinion to thinking that there are broad types of disease that pass from one to another by transmission. The former of these is the one Beza calls "absurd and against all reason."

so contrary to humanity that, as they are utter enemies to each other, so (like the disagreeing brothers) they are both in opposition to Christian community and charity. To say more were too great a wrong to the judicious Beza and to anticipate Your Honor's judgement. I commend the author to your noble approbation and hope from your noble candor, you will easily censure this presumption in,

Honorable Sir,

Your Honor's most devoted (though unknown), and most humble Servant,

Edward Percivall.

PREFACE

I CONFESS myself to have been so unacquainted with this question (whether the plague ought to be regarded as infectious) that until these past few years I had believed it never to have been doubted. But that this sickness in particular among all others was to be judged contagious, for testimony whereof before any man that is not given to quarrel I refer myself to the judgement of the writers of all countries who have treated of these things. But now in our times men have taken in hand to dispute this question upon this occasion, that many do so greatly fear this disease and the death which commonly follows the same that, forsaking all duties, not only of Christians, but also of humanity, they have greatly increased the very wrath of God, which is the chief cause of this sickness. And there has in a manner been no stay or let in them. But where this great misery has happened, the bonds of Man's fellowships being once broken, it is much to be wondered at that all Mankind has not perished and been destroyed. These men being demanded what they can allege for so impious a crime commonly bring nothing else for their excuse but the fear of infection. Thus, it has come to pass that those in whom there is a greater boldness do think that they can in no other way remedy this evil than by teaching that this sickness is falsely supposed to be infectious.

I do judge that this fear, which brings with it a forgetfulness of all duty, both may and also ought to be put away. But because I think that this paradox or strange opinion can no more be proved by good reason than if a man with Anaxagoras should hold the snow to be black or out of the hypothesis of Copernicus labor to prove that the earth does really move and the sun stand still as the center of the world, this fear ought to be put away in some other manner. Neither will I believe this disease not to be infectious until some man shall teach me either out of the Word of God or by evident and good reasons to the contrary. For there are in the very course of Nature certain and most sure grounds and proofs of this truth, so long as the order of necessary causes agree with themselves. For I deny that the station in which God has placed every man is to be forsaken even though all agree that the plague, of all other diseases, is most infectious, yea more, that unavoidable death for the most part does swiftly follow.

I deny, I say, that therefore that which we owe unto God, to our Country, and which we owe unto men, either for some public or private respect, is not to be preferred before life itself. And I had rather they would bestow their endeavors in persuasive disputes, to restrain men's flying away for fear of the plague, than that they should labor to prove their strange opinion that the plague is not infectious. Indeed, I had rather have the consequent (according to the School-phrase) in that same enthymeme to be denied than the antecedent; for by that means something might be brought to pass, not only by probable, but also by necessary arguments, according to their own desire.[2] Namely, that those do very greatly offend,

---

2. Beza is here assuming the distinction between inductive and deductive reasoning. Induction collects data by research and builds either a strong or weak inference from the collected data. Deduction takes premises and draws out (*deducere*: to lead down from; draw out) conclusions from the premises. Induction can never be certain and can only give us a probable conclusion. Deduction, by its nature, gives us necessary conclusions from the premises. This is reflected in WCF 1.6 when the divines speak of a "good and *necessary* consequence." They are speaking of deducing necessary conclusions from the premises that Scripture provides. These conclusions are necessary because, if the premises are true, the conclusion is also.

Beza also mentions three terms in this sentence that refer to formal logic: *consequent*, *enthymeme*, and *antecedent*. A *consequent* is the member of a conditional statement that follows the "then." Here is an example with the consequent underlined: "If the Bible is inspired, then <u>it is the Word of God</u>." An *antecedent* is the prior member of a conditional statement that precedes the "then." Again, here is an example with the antecedent underlined: "<u>If the Bible is inspired</u>, then it is the Word of God." An *enthymeme* is a syllogism with an assumed, and thus not ex-who for fear of any peril do offend against God, or against their neighbor. For what Christian man dares to call these things into controversy? Or if he does indeed dare, shall [he] not be reproved by the testimony of his own conscience, though all the world should be silent? For I do not think that there is any which hold that, with a good conscience, the plague by all means without exception is to be fled from, which notwithstanding I see by some in such sort disputed against as if it were by others maintained. Yet, if there be any of that mind, I do not favor their error any more than I allow of those men, which of a clean contrary opinion do think that the plague is not to be fled from. But surely it is the part of a wise man to follow the golden mean, so that he fly not when he should tarry, neither when he should go aside (for the term of flying away in this argument seems to me to be very improper) offend against that self-same charity by his

plicitly stated, premise: "New Yorkers are rude. Donald Trump is rude." The assumed premise here is "Donald Trump is a New Yorker." It is not explicitly stated and thus the syllogism is called an *enthymeme*.

The enthymeme that Beza is interacting with in this section seems to be something like this: *"If the plague is infectious, then we must flee though that causes us to abandon our duty."* Thus, the consequent that he would prefer to deny would be "we must flee though that causes us to abandon our duty." And the antecedent that some deny would be "The plague is infectious."

rash tarrying, though charity seemed to counsel him to stay.

These things I thought good in manner of a preface to set down before I come to the handling of the matter, to the end that all men at the first entrance may perceive what I have undertaken to defend and what to disprove.

WHETHER THE PLAGUE BE INFECTIOUS

SEEING THAT there are some which think that this discourse concerning the fleeing or not fleeing from the plague depends upon whether the plague is infectious or not, let us examine with what reasons and arguments they so boldly deny the plague to be infectious, a thing which hitherto by all men without controversy has been believed.

For the better determining of this question, they would have us consider what the plague is, from whence it comes, what is the cause of it, by what means it is sent unto us, what is the nature of it, and what the end. I take their proposals, for they are most lawful and reasonable. But how shall we come to the knowledge of these things? "By no means," they say, "from any reasons out of physick[3], but only by the word of God."[4] [Well] then, let all things disputed by physicians

3. I retain the old term "physick" as it more readily connects Beza's arguments about this branch of knowledge with its practitioners, "physicians."
4. I have added quotation marks to demarcate where Beza presents an argument from his interlocutor. This was not a conven-

be blotted out. Instead of the books of Hippocrates, Galen, and others, let physicians read only the Bible. In addition, let there be no difference between them and theologians, between the physick of the body and the soul.

"Nay, God forbid," they will say, "for we condemn no other reasons of physick than such as are against the word of God." Let us enquire then (forasmuch as infection has its beginning from natural causes and therefore proceeds from them) whether concerning natural causes of the plague there be anything taught in the word of God contrary to the rules and judgement of physicians. They say that the plague is called by the Hebraists *dener*, from the word *daner*, which also signifies to destroy by sentence given by God, and that the Grecians do render it *thanaton*, that is to say, death. Even so, it is not to the point. For it does not follow that the plague proceeds not from natural causes coming between, because it is sent by God. unless we are willing to take away every natural cause of disease, because no man dies, except by God decreeing the type and manner of death by which he dies.

"Nay," they say, "it is a folly to call the sentence of God, whereby he appoints unto every man, not only death itself, but also the kind of death and the secondary causes there-

---

tion in 1665 nor in the original Latin, but it has become common practice today. The convention in earlier times was merely to insert *inquit* or *inquiunt*, he says or they say.

of, infections." But who, I pray, was ever so softheaded as to call the sentence of God itself infectious? But that which we say is far otherwise: namely, that the infection itself is to be reckoned among second causes. For who can deny that many diseases are contracted by handling and touching, some of which are deadly and others less so? Unless they will also contend that the sun doesn't shine at noonday. Sin indeed, with which we are all born infected, and from which all this dying arises, by a certain spiritual infection, not without the decree of God, is conveyed and spread into all the posterity of Adam. Therefore, there is no substance at all in this reason.

But they also demand, "If infection be reckoned among second causes appointed by God, how we can avoid that which is ordained by God?" From this they hope to gather that if the plague be granted to be infectious, then in vain a remedy is sought against it by flying away. But this is also a very dull reason. For if this reason be good, shall it not be lawful to affirm the same of all second causes of death? If so, "Let us neither eat, nor drink, nor seek any remedy against any diseases!" (1 Cor. 15:32). Let soldiers go unarmed to battle, because death ordained by God cannot be avoided. But this is actually the case: doubtless neither death, nor the time, nor any kind of death appointed by God can be avoided. Neither do we eat, nor use remedies against diseases, nor put on armor against our enemies as if we meant to withstand God. But leaving those things which God would have kept secret from us, we must use those things which, God himself going before, nature tells us are ordained by him to prolong our life so long as it shall please him. Which if we do not, we shall rightly be deemed to tempt and most grievously offend God. So far off is it that using the means set down by him to avoid death we should sin against him. [For,] even though we sometimes use them in vain, that is to say that even so we must die, when as we thought our life should yet for a time have been prolonged. Thus was Asa rebuked, not because he sent for physicians, but because he put his hope of life in the physicians (2 Chron. 16:12). So then, when experience has taught us that infection creeps rather into things near than afar off, he is not to be accused who leaving no part of Christian duty undone withdraws himself and his family. Nay, he shall be greatly blamed who rashly casts himself and his into the danger of infection. When, as the Apostle bears witness, he is worse than an infidel which has not so great care over his as with a pious safety and charity he ought to have (1 Tim. 5:8).

Now let us see whether this following reason be of any more force. "By those names," they say, "which in the Holy Scripture are attributed to the plague, it is sufficiently and thoroughly expressed what the quality and manner of the same is. Now the plague is called the hand of God (2 Sam.

24:14-15), the word of God (1 Chron. 21), and is also signified by the name of arrows (Ps. 31; 91:5-6). Therefore, it comes not by infection. For neither hand, nor sword, nor arrow, wounds by infection." But besides that, perhaps I might rightly call into doubt whether all these testimonies alleged deny this argument also. For in another place, such as Psalm 17:14 (KJV), David calls his enemies "the hand of God," who by natural means assaulted him. And when the hand of God is said to have made us, natural generation is not left out. It is manifest that in the Scripture all evils and punishments whatsoever God sends upon mankind, using either the ordinary laws of nature or the service of angels, are called "arrows." I demand moreover, what they call the quality and manner of the disease. They will say, "The nature thereof itself." But I say by those metaphorical terms of "hand," "sword," and "arrow" it is no more signified of what manner or quality this disease is in itself than what the hail or scab is when God is said with a stretched out hand to have smitten Egypt (Ex. 9:18, Deut. 28:27). And, to be short, what is the force and nature of every disease when in the additions of the Law they are reckoned up among the curses which God would send upon them (Deut. 28:15-68)?

What then? Surely then, it belongs to the physicians to search out the nature of diseases, so far as they depend upon the laws of nature, which we often see performed by them with such good success and certainty that they can predict both them and what issue they are likely to come to. But concerning supernatural and divine causes of sickness and other miseries, those do theologians declare, teaching that we must mount far above nature and all things appertaining unto nature, when with our prayers we deal with the avoiding and removing of them far away from us. For the true and principal cause of them is our sins. God, being provoked therewith, raises and stirs up against us all these inferior causes, to be revenged on mankind with just punishments. I therefore say that it is an absurd and foolish thing to confound these things, so distinct and distinguished by their diverse yet not contrary ends, save that they are placed the one under the other.

And because in this argument, they contend that the plague therefore is not infectious, for it is often called the hand, and sword, and arrow of God, I demand of them whether leprosy was not the hand of God and not therefore infectious. Further, because it was infectious, whether therefore the lepers were not commanded to depart aside from the rest that were clean? I demand this also, if there be an evil in the city which the Lord has not done (Amos 3:6)? Whether today, notwithstanding, the foul black spotty and scurvy leprosy called elephantiasis should not be considered infectious? And I would gladly ask of them which find fault with our going aside during plague, whether they think that those which are infected should be allowed in the common company and society of men? And if they suppose that they should be allowed, why they do not also find fault and call out those who shut them out? If not, and think that they should be avoided for fear of the infection, why without all exceptions do they blame those that shun the infections of the plague as the most hurtful to all persons?

But they will perhaps deny that that kind of leprosy is the hand of God. Let us speak of the pox, whether it be the French or the Spanish, I would to God it were not also the English. That it is a punishment sent from God for whoredom, which in these times is accounted as a sportive recreation, I think there is no man which dares to deny that it is indeed the hand, sword, or arrow of God which strikes whoremongers. But is it not therefore infectious? And does not a whore even infect many with this disease, who again expose one another? So that this most filthy sickness is contracted, not only by lying together, but also by breathing and handling, and is sucked out by infants from their nurse's breasts. And the nurses get this disease by giving suck unto the infant which is either conceived by an unclean father or born of an unclean mother. Those arguments also are such as need no confutation. Without all question it is absurd and against all reason to think that there are immediately (as they say) sent unto every man in particular so many particular plagues, rather than kinds of disease which one harms another by infection. For whether God kill at one stroke, or whether, as it fell out unto the Midianites, he strike them down by one wounding another whomsoever he has appointed to die, what difference is there? Neither concerning what we have in hand is there any difference, whether any man be slain with the dart of God himself or the infection of another.

Let us now come unto that which they allege concerning second causes, which they deny to be any certain placing of the stars or corruption of the air. Neither will the physicians have any plague or infection to grow of those causes. But if we grant this and imagine that all natural causes of the plague are [comprehended under these two (air and stars)], they must tell me why they shut out all these at once, since they reckon them to have but small skill in the Scriptures, who impute the plague (next after God) to these causes? "Because," they say, "that the Holy Scriptures bear record, that the plague is sent by angels, as Psalm 88, 1 Chron. 21, Ezek. 9 [bear witness]; also, in the history of Sennacherib (Is. 37:36), and in the Revelation (16:1-2) where there is mention made of a most noisome ulcer. For," they say, "that which God sends by angels is not of natural causes." I grant that, so far as [it] concerns the angels themselves, whom I agree are not reckoned among natural instruments. But what hinders, God so commanding, the natural causes themselves to be stirred up by the angels? For surely it cannot be doubted that they, both the good and the bad, do stir up the mind of man after a certain sort, whatsoever kind of moving it be. For instance, Satan is said to have entered into the heart of Judas (Luke 22:3), (unless we shall peradventure say that the good angels have somewhat less power than the bad) and that also is manifest in the story of Ahab, by the efficacy and power of the spirits of error (1 Kings 22:19-22). And who can deny that the will of man is to be reckoned among the supreme causes of men's actions? But if the will of man is not debarred from the ministry of angels, why should we think that other natural causes must needs by the same be taken away? Moses, stretching forth his rod, raised up lice and innumerable sorts of flies, brought out the sudden fearful hail, and struck the Egyptians with most noisome boils and botches (Ex 8:16, 24, 9:10, 23). And this ministry of Moses was doubtless altogether as extraordinary as the ministry of angels. But did not therefore the lice and flies come of rottenness? The hail from vapors growing together on the sudden by restraint of the contrary? And the boils and botches also from corruptions of the humors? Satan, receiving a grant from God, by suddenly raising the wind and by throwing abroad fire from heaven overthrew and burnt the house of Job, together with all his children (Job 1:12-19). But does it therefore follow that this came to pass without any natural causes stepping in between? Or shall we not rather say that those princes of the air, as the Apostle not without cause calls them (Eph. 2:2), made in a moment those truly natural impressions of the air? The devil sends the godly to prison (Rev. 2:10), but by tyrants and persecutors of the Church. In the same book (6: 8) the pale horse on whom Death the rider sits receives power to kill with the sword, famine, and pestilence, and sending of wild beasts. Here, if we shall by that rider understand an angel, why shall we not as well say that he used natural matter to cause the plague and famine, as a sword and wild beasts, when [they] themselves are also natural instruments? And afterwards, (9: 1), the angels are commanded to stand in the four quarters of the earth and to keep back the winds, that they hurt not the sea and the land with blowing. Whereof it follows that at the commandment of God the winds are in like manner sent forth by them, from the which doubtless it is manifest that many infections of the air and chiefly infection proceeds. So that natural causes, whether they be moved by little and little of their own force planted in them by nature, or otherwise beyond order, God so commanding, they be in a moment carried to their effects, they are natural. Likewise, their effects are also rightly judged natural, which no man of reason can deny.

For if there come in no natural causes in the plague, those whom the plague has touched doubtless cannot be at all eased, much less be healed by natural remedies. And to prove this to be most false, experience and very sense demonstrate. Yet I profess myself to be one of those which does so far detest the superstitious judicious astrology, or casters of nativities, and all other such like predictions, that I could wish the old statutes of princes concerning those things were renewed and strictly observed. But to remove from the divers concourses of the stars, the natural constitutions of the air, and such effects as depend upon them in our bodies, as if the stars were only placed in their spheres to be looked upon or for difference of times, I think to be no sign of discernment, but rather of a perverse stubbornness, since the husbandmen have a daily knowledge of this and the tempests do speak the same. And the thing itself proves that the temperature and distemperature, and even infection itself in some measure may be predicted by skillful astrologers.[5]

But now should we grant that those plagues, the ex-

---

5. That the reader be not too put off by Beza's discussion of astrology and the effects that the stars have upon earth, consider the Moon. We recognize that the moon produces effects upon earth: the tides. While I do not agree with Beza's particular view on astrology, we need not become chronological elites thinking he lived in a benighted age. His main point is to show the relationship between secondary causes.

amples whereof are taken out of Holy Scripture, were sent by angels and therefore to have been without infection, why should it be less absurd and against reason to conjecture and resolve that no plague is sent by angels, than to hold that no hail, no showers, no lightning is made by the course of nature? Because that in many places of the Scriptures we read that by the ministry of angels it has both hailed and that most rough and blustering winds have blown and that it has horribly thundered. "But," they say, "those examples of the plague by angels are set forth unto us for example that thereby we may learn rightly to judge concerning middle causes and of the original of the plague." Truly who will deny that what things soever are written are written for our instruction (Rom 15:4), and that all things which are mentioned in the Holy Scriptures of the ministry of angels, not only of the plague, but also of famine and other calamities, both to destroy the wicked, and also to correct and exercise the good, brings unto us great profit? Namely, that we may learn both to fear and love God, who is not tied unto the laws of nature, as the Stoic philosophers have thought, and has certain instruments of his judgements more fearful even that those which are perceived by our senses. But hereby is not concluded that which you would have, namely, that thus we are taught that there are no natural causes used by angels in the performance of the commandments of God. The Scripture affords us examples of plague sent upon men, making no mention of angels. And those, against whom I dispute, grant that it was the plague of which Hezekiah was sick, yet he is not said to have been stricken by angels. God often, by Moses and other prophets, threatens the plague unto sinners. Neither is there any doubt but that these threatenings were not in vain. Yet he nowhere recites that he will always send them by angels. The Psalmist seems in certain Psalms to show that he was taken with the plague. Notwithstanding we never read that he was struck with any sore or wound given by the angels. All these things therefore, unless I be very much deceived, have no bearing at all on taking away the contagious air, the second cause of this sickness.

But this also they set down, upon what reason I know not how grounded. They say that "the plague is sent unto men by the singular and especial providence of God." And what is here which may not be affirmed of everything which comes to pass in the world? "For," as he says, "not so much as a sparrow falls to the earth without the providence of God, and the hairs of our head are numbered" (Matt. 10:28-31). This providence, if it be stretched unto particular things, doubtless it is in such sort universal in the general, that it is also singular in the particular. They say, moreover, that "so often as the plague reigns in the world, that all those are kept from this infection whom God has appointed to preserve alive, and that unto the others all places are infectious, though they be far removed from those which are sick of the plague." And they add further and say, "Why then do we fear infection? Is it not a foolish thing to fear that which is not?" I for my part cannot discern how these things can hang together. For how can all places be infectious to any man, if there be no infection,[6] unless peradventure they reject it to be the case? But it cannot by any means truly be gathered by certainty of God's providence that the plague is not infectious. Therefore, this argument runs beyond the question propounded.

Besides, shall we think that the number of those which shall die is more certain as often as God sends the plague than when he casts other darts? Now if they, who use remedies of physick both preservative and sanitary to keep away sickness and also to heal when it comes, offend not against the providence of God, (who leaving, as it is meet, things unknown unto us to the good will and pleasure of himself), why should we do the like also in the heat of the plague? As therefore God has appointed some which shall not die of the plague, so also has he appointed the remedies by which, so

6. Interestingly, this is the same kind of refutation employed against transubstantiation. The real argument over the presence of Christ in the Supper is an argument over the accidents of the bread and wine and the causal relationship between them and our senses.

far as in them lieth, men may avoid the plague. And it is one and the same providence of God in all kind of diseases which he has ordained by an unchangeable decree what shall come to pass, although the natures of the diseases differ widely in themselves.

Now among the chief remedies and provisions in physick against infection, "going aside" in due season is rightly reckoned, [as] the very nature and signification of the word "contagion"[7] declares. Even though neither are all saved which fly, neither do all die which tarry. God without all doubt when he sent a famine into Egypt and the regions roundabout had determined who should die in that scarcity. Yet for all this Joseph ceased not with the best diligence and most wise counsel to provide for the Egyptians (Gen. 41:25-49). Likewise, the Churches in the time of Claudius the Emperor also did, when as they understood by Agabus the prophet that a famine should shortly come (Acts 11:28-30). The Lord also knew who should die in that most cruel war of the Assyrians in the days of Hezekiah, and yet both

7. *Contagio, contagionis* – a touching or contact (D. P. Simpson, *Cassell's Latin Dictionary*, fifth edition [New York: Wiley Publishing, 1968], 145). Beza makes good use of this term to prove that "turning aside" is a remedy in times of contagion which literally means "touch" or "contact." This is an example of argument from definition. He will bring this point up in at least two more places.

Hezekiah and the prophet Isaiah himself secured themselves within the walls of the city (2 Chron 32:1-5). What should I say more? When Paul knew assuredly that neither he himself, neither any of those which were with him would perish in the shipwreck, yet said he to the mariners who were preparing to fly out of the ship, "Ye cannot be saved unless these tarry" (Acts 27:31). Christ also, though he well knew that his hour was not yet come, yet did he more than once withdraw himself when the Jews sought to kill him.

Finally, that which they take for most certain, namely, that happening or chance is repugnant unto the sure and steadfast decree of God, which, notwithstanding, it makes no difference to the matter, yet who will grant it them? We call those happening or chancing causes which of their own nature may fall out unto either part. If any man should take them out of the nature of things, I know not whether he should have any man of a right judgment to hold with him. They say out of St. Augustine that "the will of God is the necessity of things." I grant this so far as it pertains unto the end and effects of the causes themselves. But as St. Augustine says very well, "It follows not that though all things which God has decreed shall come to pass must needs come to pass that therefore they come to pass of necessary causes," just as the Stoics falsely concluded, and the same may be proved by most certain and most plain examples. For, do we not believe that Christ had indeed man's bones and therefore, such as of their own nature might at any time have been broken? And yet indeed they could not be broken, for, it was otherwise decreed by God (Ps 34:20; John 19:36). Therefore, by hap and chance, concerning their own nature they were not broken, when as notwithstanding they were such as might have been broken, and yet by God's decree they remained of necessity unbroken. Again, that Christ from the very time that he took upon him our human nature was endued with a mortal body, all Christians do confess. Therefore, of his own nature he might have been slain by Herod with the other little children (Matt 2:16-18). But by God's decree he could not. Therefore, that he was not then slain fell out by hap and chance, if you consider the nature of his body, when as it might have chanced otherwise. But, by God's decree, he could no more be slain by Herod than the will of God could be changed. Christ, when he was carried to be crucified, was then undoubtedly of such health that he needed not at that time to have died. He died therefore by chance, if you do consider the cause of his natural death. And yet he died of necessity, if you look to the unchangeable appointment of his Father, because his hour was come. And withal he died willingly, because he laid down his life for us. Thus far therefore is neither chance nor will repugnant to the most certain decree of God.

There remains one argument taken from experience, which seems very strong on the surface, yet is it of no force to prove that the plague is not infectious. "If," they say, "the plague comes of natural causes, or of some certain constellation, or of corrupt air, then should all they doubtless be infected which dwell under the same constellation or breathe in the same corrupt air," which is found to be false: for even reason itself proves the falsehood of this argument. For who is so unskillful that knows not that one and the same cause does not always operate alike, much less equally, nay, that the effects are diverse, according to the diversity of the matter it acts upon. The selfsame north wind does not equally annoy men with cold. Everyone therefore sees how weak this reason is. But let us grant that in some place every man of himself is apt to receive the corrupt air, yet many things may happen which would hinder the same effect following in all; as, for example, one man takes a preservative medicine, another doesn't. One immediately uses a good medicine; another very late, or never.

Lastly, that which is the principal point is to be considered: Almighty God governs natural causes and their effects as it pleases him. So that hence it comes to pass that infection touches not everyone which is in danger of it, as it is written (Ps. 91:6). Neither yet is it deadly unto everyone that it has infected, just as poison is not, as it is written (Mark

16:18). Therefore, this argument also is not of force to prove there is no infection in the plague, because that many which keep company with those that are sick of the plague are not taken. And contrariwise, they that are absent are infected, as if the poison of a viper were not deadly because Paul being bitten by one felt no harm at all (Acts 28:5).

And thus far concerning infection.

THREE

WHETHER AND HOW FAR IT MAY BE SHUNNED OF CHRISTIANS BY GOING ASIDE

NOW WE must treat of going aside. For so I had rather call it than flying, though I think it the part of a wise man to fly peril with reason. There are some, therefore, which do without exception find fault with going aside for the plague, that they count it a very heinous offense, even though they think that those who tarry ought not to use rashness. There are, on the other side which hold that every man, so soon as the plague comes, ought to provide for himself with little or no regard for the fellowship and duties which Christian charity commands. Now I, for my part, dissent from both these and especially from the latter as having most lawful causes. But before I set down my own judgement in this controversy, let us hear these disputing the one against the other.

Thus, they which think it not lawful to fly, in the first

place, philosophically dispute against those that hold it not lawful to tarry at all. They allege, out of Plato's *Gorgias* that "it is foolishness to fear death. And that he cannot be regarded as a temperate person which flees death, because it proceeds from too much delight in life. Nor yet to be a just man, since he which in the time of the plague provides for himself by running away yields neither to God nor man his due." To these reasons they set down others taken out of the Holy Scriptures, such as that they think not well of the providence of God, by whose unchangeable decree the course of man's life is limited; that they distrust God, and believe not his promise, "I will be thy God, and the God of thy seed"; that they are void of all charity, nay, and more, of all natural pity and affection; that they tempt God after the example of the Israelites (Ex. 17:3, Ps. 78:18) appointing God by what manner, time, place, and the means by which he may save them; that they love not God from their hearts, for being enamored and in love with earthly goods, they neglect and are careless of the heavenly; that they fear death too much, for that they set themselves against the will of God which is always good; that they think themselves stronger than God, and that they can escape his hand; that they do openly break the law of Christ and of nature, by which they are commanded to do unto others as they would have done unto themselves; that they do, and teach that which no Christian has done, but that which has often been done by the heathens.

And this much say the first, unto whom these later have nothing to answer, who under pretense of saving their lives, argue for flying away without exception. Wherefore if the things alleged against those which fly from the plague, so that they swerve at all from the rules and laws of godliness and charity, I hold with their adversaries, and count them worthy of all blame, which fly from thence whither they should run, if they had but the least spark of humanity. But if these reasons be used against those who, being moved with just causes, go aside and keep that mean by which they fail in no part of their duty either towards God or their neighbors (which may oftentimes be done), we affirm that all these arguments, however plausible and strong they appear, to be of no force or value, if the matter itself be diligently weighed and considered. For in answer to their first reason, albeit the decree of God be unchangeable and that his eternal providence has set the unremovable bounds of our lives, yet this does not take away the ordinary and lawful means to save our lives, no, not even if a man has received an answer from God of prolonging his life, as we have shown by the manifest example of Saint Paul (Acts 27:24, 31), much less that we may not use these means when it is yet hid from us what God from everlasting has decreed concerning the prolonging and ending of our life. Moreover, why should he be said to distrust the promises of God who follows the ways appointed by God to avoid evils, that notwithstanding he depends wholly upon God? Unless peradventure we can anywhere find in the Holy Scriptures this commandment expressly written, "When the plague rages, fly not away," and among those ways, preservative remedies are to be reckoned, among those remedies, going aside in due time, as the very name "contagion" manifests. And this also is plain that he does not only not offend against Christian charity, nor yet tempt God, who in such manner by going aside avoids the plague, so that in the meantime he let pass no act of piety towards God, or of charity towards his neighbor. On the contrary, unless he performs these duties, he may be thought to provoke the wrath of God against himself, and to be worse than an infidel, as being one that rashly puts himself in danger of deadly infection, without any care of himself or his.

The fifth and sixth allegation is not any whit truer. "They love not God," they say, "and, gaping after earthly things, they care not for heavenly. Because they which love God desire nothing more than to be with him, which falls out unto us by death. But they, which love God, on the contrary fear nothing more." Then truly he, who in loving has only his last end before any other for his own profit to enjoy the thing he loves by what means so ever it be shall rightly be judged to love himself rather than his friends. Therefore, the self-same person [the Apostle Paul] which desires to be loosed and to be with Christ, wishes also for his brethren's sake to be separated as a thing accursed (Romans 9:3). Neither does he deliver up his life into the hands of them that lay in wait for him, appealing unto Caesar (Acts 25:2-11) and gives thanks for his health restored unto him (2 Cor. 1:11). David also does not so much fly from Saul and Absalom, as death, being notwithstanding a worshipper of God. He and Hezekiah do expressly pray against death. Therefore, whosoever flies from death is not rashly to be judged or censured as not loving God. On the contrary, whosoever desires death is not to be thought to love God, but only he who, lawfully and with a good conscience in obeying the will of God prepares himself either to suffer or avoid death. The like also is to be judged of the fear of death. That is, if it be grounded upon good reason and moderately, it is not only not to be condemned, but also to be allowed as a preserver of life ingrained in us by God. Therefore, that fear of evil is condemned by philosophers, which is contrary to fortitude, and calls us from that which every one of us owes unto each other. Holy Scripture likewise condemns that fear which is against faith and charity. For it is one thing to take clean away natural affections, (which no man could ever possibly do) and another to moderate and rule them. The Philosophers ably teach that this ought to be done. But how it may be done, the Word of God by the Holy Ghost only declares.

And concerning those things which they cite out of Tertullian, they shoot partly beyond his mark when he speaks of flying only in persecution. Partly also those things from Tertullian, with wide consent of the Church, are reckoned among his blemishes, as one that in this argument was carried beyond the butt.[8] No man that is undoubtedly godly and of right understanding ever condemned the going aside of Jacob. No man ever condemned David flying the fury of Saul and conspiracy of Absalom, nor Elijah avoiding by his flight the rage of Jezebel. No man ever condemned the going aside of Athanasius more than once. Neither do we here fly either unto the agony of Christ or unto that of Matthew 10:23, "If they persecute you in one city, fly unto another," which passages, I confess, are of some not rightly applied. For, concerning the fears of Christ, they are grounded upon a peculiar consideration, and are not to be drawn into example. Since in that passage the mystery of our salvation is handled,

---

8. This is an apt metaphor that Beza uses that could also be attributed to Mr. Percival's translator. The use of the term "butt" here is in reference to a small mound of earth upon which an archery target would be supported. Marksmanship was a common pastime in the England of Mr. Percival's day and continues to have a place in America. Thus, "to be carried beyond the butt" would be equivalent to our "overshooting" or "missing the target."

the parts whereof Christ alone both could and did take upon him, in the which he did see that fearful wrath of his Father, and indeed felt it, bearing the punishment due unto our sins. We on the contrary are not at our deaths tried with the same fears, because we have the Father appeased with us, and, through faith, behold life in death itself. And that saying of Christ is doubtless no command of flying away, but on the contrary, admonishes faithful pastors that, being afraid of no threatenings, if they be driven out of one place, they hasten unto another, the which afterwards we see diligently to have been done by the Apostles.

But let us hear something else of more weight perhaps, "There can be nothing sent of God," they say, "but that which is good. Nay, there is nothing good, but that which comes from God. But the plague is sent of God, therefore it is good; if not of its own nature, yet in respect of the good end, namely, to punish our sins, to try our faith, to drive us to repentance, and to bring forth hypocrites to light. Who therefore," they say, "can deny, but that they fly the thing that is good, which fly the plague, by the which God bringeth all these things to pass?" Again, "That which God sends upon all, that is to say, upon any one church or kingdom, [such] as for example, the plague, the same he will have born of all. How is it to be fled from? Therefore, they set themselves against the will of God who fly the plague. Nay, they fly in vain, because it is in vain to strive against the will of God." But what could have been more vainly said than these things? For, to let pass the falsehood that crouches in these words "good" and "evil" in this argument, to what end I pray you should they enter into this disputation concerning the nature of things? There is no evil (that is to say, no calamity or punishment) in the city which the Lord has not done says the prophet (Amos 3:6). Why therefore should we call famine, pestilence, war, and such like, good? "Yes. Because," they say, "they fall out unto the good of the godly." I grant it, because the Lord fetches light out of darkness. Yea, but the godly are instructed by sin itself. Are sins, I pray you, therefore good, and does he which resists them resist God? To be short, who sees not that to pray unto God against things which of their own nature are harmful, and to use just and lawful remedies to avoid them, if at all possible, and so trusting God for the result, to be a far other thing than it is, or that we should hope to withstand God or by any means to escape his judgements? Abraham himself, Isaac, and Jacob did fly hunger, which notwithstanding was sent of God. And yet they cannot be said to have fled the thing that was good or to have sinned.

As for that which they so greatly stand upon, namely that "those which fly the plague do break that immoveable precept which humanity itself teaches, 'Whatsoever ye would that men should do unto you, do ye the same unto them,'" as it is rightly turned upon them which do in this way fly the plague, or any other danger, that thus neglect the duties of a Christian. Likewise, it does not apply to them who shun the plague by going aside, unless they may be judged to have neglected to perform those duties which they owe both unto their country and to their neighbor. And truly, I do marvel that those who without exception condemn going aside as being of itself repugnant unto charity, do not consider that charity more so requires that we help those that are taken with that sickness, than that we provide for the whole.

Finally, they say that "as many as fly the plague, do that which no Christian ever did, since there is no example thereof in the holy histories." I answer that this is too deceitful an argument, since it is apparent that in the Holy Scriptures it is not set down what everyone has done, and that in many [passages], [according to] the general rules of doctrine, there is sufficient to determine those things whereof we have no commandment, nor any particular example, and that it is without doubt that it is not set down how often the people were visited with the plague nor how every man behaved himself in the plague. But they say they have altogether contrary counsel in the Holy Scriptures. For "David calls us back unto the Tabernacle of the Most High (Psalm 91)" as though he fled not unto God, which lawfully uses going aside. "But yet" they say, "David did not fly that very sore plague whereof mention is made (2 Sam. 24), neither did he remove his household unto any other place." I grant this. But how many peculiar circumstances forbid us to draw out a general conclusion from that episode? For he himself was the cause of that plague, and being rightly troubled by it, he was ready, even with his own destruction, to redeem the public calamity. Further, when as this plague continued not above three days at the most, what place was there left for him to take advice or to fly unto? Whither should he have fled, when the plague was hot in all his dominion, and yet is said not at all, or very little, to have touched the chief city itself? Again, they say, "Isaiah fled not from Hezekiah being sick of the plague." As if we held that the shepherds with a good conscience might willingly, and of their own accord, leave their sheep. Yea, and what if I should point out that Isaiah came not to Hezekiah but by the special command of God? For so the history bears record (2 Kings 20:4-5). "But," say they, "Jeremiah also, and Baruch, with other godly men, fled not out of the city being besieged of the Chaldees, though a great part of the people died of the plague as well as famine." Neither do we say that we may rightly shun the plague by going aside if we depart from that which we owe unto God, our country, and each of our neighbors. But I cannot but wonder that those which allege this example of Jeremiah have forgotten that he was taken at the gate of the city trying to get out (Jer. 37:11-13).

Last of all, they bring a notable example of the Church of Alexandria out of the seventh book of Eusebius, chapter 20, as though we granted the going aside either of all, or in all places and times, and do not teach that such constancy and charity ought both to be praised and followed such that a hard and fast principle be not made thereof. For Eusebius does not say that every, but that very many of the Christians did it.

Therefore, to conclude these things, there has been nothing yet alleged whereby the plague has been proved either not to be infectious or that going aside to avoid infection is without exception to be condemned. That going aside is one of the chief natural remedies and provisions in infectious diseases, reason and experience itself teaches. For doubtless the word "contagion" itself loudly proclaims this, namely, that those things which are less far off are more in danger of it. It is daily observed that by removing in due time unto more healthful places many have been preserved, which if any man will except against, would have been saved if they had tarried still at home, because God had so decreed. What then shall he say who agrees not also with other shunnings and remedies of all perils? Therefore, we ought to laugh at, as needless, not only physick, but also all prudence and wisdom which is used in avoiding dangers of all sorts. Neither should there be any difference between rashness and discretion, between fortitude and boldness. But the matter is far otherwise, because like as God by his everlasting and unchangeable decree has appointed the course of our life, so has he also ordained middle causes, which we should use to preserve our lives.

FOUR

PRACTICAL COUNSEL AND APPLICATION OF THE DOCTRINE[9]

IT NOW remains that I show you when it may be convenient to go aside. For as in other indifferent things, so also a man may use going aside both well and ill. Far be it from me to enjoin the same rule upon every man without exception. On the contrary, I confess that they offend less who, when they might have withdrawn themselves with a good conscience, venture and endanger their lives by tarrying, rather than appear to forsake their neighbor or family. I confess, I say, that these offend much less than those who, being carried away with too much distrust or with an unmeasurable fear of death, forgetting and neglecting all duties of humanity, have this only before their eyes, "Away quickly, a far off, long ere you return again." These men, surely, are most worthy to be thrust out of the company of men, whose bonds they shatter to pieces.

9. This section head is not part of the original. I have added it for clarity.

Now, I think that which ought to be borne in mind under this head may best be determined in the following manner.

First of all, I think it is to be provided that every man summon himself to the judgement seat of God, regarding the plague as a foretaste of the wrath of God, and condemn himself, that he may be acquitted by him, and withal that he duly consider with himself that he is called to stand forth, plead his own cause (Job 40:1-2, 6-7), and that this rod cannot be avoided by change of place, but of manners, and that if he must die, that this is decreed for the good of them which die, forasmuch as they are blessed which die in the Lord.

Secondly, that no man either go aside or tarry with a doubtful conscience. Rather, when he has learned out of the Word of God what his duty is, he commend himself unto God and continue constantly therein. Although in so great a variety of circumstances rules for every single thing cannot be set down, yet is it no hard matter to give certain general precepts agreeable to the Word of God, by which, as by a certain rule, individual cases may afterwards (as they say) be tried. Let them therefore which think to tarry know that it is the commandment of God, "Thou shalt not Kill," (Ex. 20:13) and that therefore neither their own, nor the lives of any belonging or depending on them are rashly to be put in danger of deadly infection. Let them on the other side, which think to go away, know that no man ought to have so great a regard either of himself or of his family that he forget what one owes unto his country and fellow citizens whether they be bound by the common bond of humanity and society or by any other kind of friendship, for love seeks not the things which are her own. Wherefore I confess that I cannot see by what reason at all any man is forbidden to depart which, either by reason of age or sickness, is past hope of recovery and so cannot help others. And if they tarry, they may therefore seem only to remain that they may die, to the great loss of the commonwealth. For, their cruelty can never enough be blamed who thrust them out of their cities, especially if they be of the poor sort. And so, the pious natures of parents, in due season, providing for the preservation and life of theirs, without prejudice or hurt to any man, it seems to me, ought to be greatly commended. In addition, the providence of the magistrates is much to be praised where their care is extended (without damage to the commonwealth)[10] to see that those weak ones, as seed-beds of citizens, be well looked unto.

And here comes, by the way, that general bond where-

10. In the 1665 translation, Mr. Percival has the term "commonwelfare" here. I have changed it to "commonwealth" as that is a more common term in our day. The political use of "commonwealth" arose from this primary idea that a political organization was for the common good or "commonwelfare."

with man is especially bound unto man, which without taking away humanity itself cannot be broken. There is also another bond binding every citizen unto his country and city. But both these bonds I affirm to be natural and universal. Thus, everyone must have regard to his estate[11] and calling. For some serve in public offices, either civil or ecclesiastical; the rest are private persons. And the threads binding private persons to each other are manifold, of which nature itself is the warp and Christian godliness the woof, which, unless they be distinguished so that every man may know what his duty is in all things, it must needs follow that confusion shall bear the sway in all things under a show of order. Therefore, let man help man; citizen, citizen, that needs his help, according to his power. And let him not think of going aside if it appears likely to him that by this means somebody shall be ill looked unto. So much the more then, let him not depart any whit through contempt of any man or of an overwrought fear of death from the duty of humanity. But when, avoiding the neglect of his duty and public offense, he may be careful, both for himself and his by going aside, I see no reason why he may not simply go aside, but also why he is not bound to go aside, except in this case, that any man by flattering of

11. Here the Percival translation uses the term "estate" in the same way that the Westminster Standards use it, namely, to refer to a station or position (See WSC Q&A 12-13, 17-20). It does not refer to a man's estate as in his accumulated wealth.

himself might sin against his neighbor by going aside.

It is the duty of a Christian magistrate to provide that those things which either breed or nourish the plague be taken away as far as he is able. And that regard may be had for those that are visited with this sickness, that all be not driven to be careful for all. But how they that serve in any public civil office may leave their charge in the time of the plague, I do not see. And for faithful pastors to forsake but one poor sheep at that time when he most needs heavenly comfort is too shameful, nay too wicked a part.

As touching private persons, their bonds of friendship and amity are divers and manifold. Among these, this is chief, unto which also the natural blood bond, as God witnesses (Gen. 2:24), must give place: I mean the bond and tie of wedlock. Thus, in my judgement, the husband cannot with a good conscience go, nor the wife from the husband, especially if one of them is visited with the plague. And how much parents owe unto their children, and children to their parents, kinsmen to kinsmen, the very laws of nature declare. Christian charity is so far from letting unraveling these laws of nature that, on the contrary, it binds them the more tightly. Yea, and for servants to forsake their masters, or masters to look slenderly to their servants being sick (which cometh too often to pass), who have made use of their service when they were well, is cruelty. Yet, the bond of all these friendships is not alike or equal. Therefore, that which is not so near must give place to the nearer, even as many cannot be discharged at once.[12]

Furthermore, just as there is place also for departure among those which are present, unless they which tarry are performing some duty, so also heed is to be taken by those that are sick, that they abuse not the love of their kindred and friends, even though they desire to have themselves provided for. Also, care should be taken by those which continue in doing their duties, that they cast not themselves rashly into the danger of infection, which is common among those motivated by desperate boldness, rather than true and Christian judgement. These are such that look down upon those that are sick of other diseases, and visit those that are taken with the plague, that they may appear to despise death. This contempt of God's judgements I would tolerate far less than the weakness of the fearful. But how others are affected and disposed in the craving of the presence of their friends I know not. I myself was visited with the plague, and many of my friends offered unto me all kind of courtesy. I allowed none to come unto me, lest I be thought to have provided for myself with no regard for my friends. But if in such calamities the magistrate fails to act in a timely manner as much

12. See WLC Q&A 123-133 for a fuller treatment of the relations that nature weaves among us.

as he can, both to prevent the spread of infection and to see
that the sick of the plague lack nothing by such lawful means
as are not repugnant unto Christian charity; he, [who holds
to his duty as dictated by love],[13] shall doubtless do very well

13. In the original 1665 edition, these penultimate lines are:
"But if in such Calamities the Magistrate do not in time provide, as much as may be, both by such lawful means as are not
repugnant unto Christian Charitie, that the Infection may be
prevented, and also that the sick of the plague want nothing; he
shall doubtless do very well both for the sick & the whole, and
shall take away many Questions which in this Argument are
wont to be raised."

The antecedent of the phrase beginning with "he shall doubtless" is difficult to determine. If we suppose the magistrate of the
prior clauses (the last used nominative), the meaning becomes
non-sensical. If, however, we suppose the putative "man" whom
Beza is counseling, the meaning becomes clearer. As I have edited this sentence, I have supposed the "everyman" whom Beza is
counseling is the antecedent of the phrase "he shall doubtless."
This can be justified on the supposition that a Latinate language,
in which Beza's original was surely written, whether Latin or
French, employs nouns which carry grammatical gender. This
grammatical feature is of great value in determining antecedents
as both the noun and the pronoun carry gender. Due to this feature of the grammar and the propensity of Latinate languages to
employ participles, a vast expanse of verbal hills and dales often
interposes between a pronoun and its antecedent. Thus, have I
edited and thus have I reasoned; I leave the success up to your
judgement, candid reader.

both for the ill and the hale. He shall also remove many questions which, in this argument, are want to be raised.

But this especially must be agreed upon, that as our sins are the chief and true cause of the plague, so that this is the only proper remedy against the same: if the ministers dispute not of the infection (which belongs to physicians) but by their life and doctrine stir up the people to earnest repentance, and love, and charity one towards another.

FINIS

This is one of the difficulties of rendering a Latinate language such as Latin or French into English. Yea, Elizabethan English is more Latinate than contemporary English, and the distance between pronouns and their antecedents is, in Percival's phrase, repugnant to charitable contemporary English style.

CPSIA information can be obtained
at www.ICGtesting.com
Printed in the USA
LVHW050159230122
709145LV00010B/1078

9 781952 410758